# Fastest Animals
# In the World

Billy Grinslott – Kinsey Marie Books

ISBN - 9781968228552

The peregrine falcon is the fastest animal in flight, and the overall fastest member of the animal kingdom. The peregrine falcon can reach speeds over 200 miles per hour during its characteristic hunting dive, or "stoop". While they usually fly at cruising speeds of 35 miles per hour, when stooping, the peregrine falcon soars to a great height, then dives steeply at speed of over 200 miles per hour. Their speed is enabled by pointed wings, stiff feathers, and a specialized, cone-shaped body that reduces drag when their wings are folded in.

Golden eagles are incredibly fast raptors, capable of reaching speeds between 150 and 200 miles per hour when diving (stooping) to hunt. Their typical cruising or soaring speed is much slower, usually around 32 miles per hour. They can, however, reach horizontal flight speeds up to 80 miles per hour. They often use their high-speed dives to hunt mammals and birds, by using their massive wingspan of up to 7 feet wide for speed and agility.

Gyrfalcons are incredibly fast, reaching speeds of up to 130 miles per hour in a dive (a stoop). But they are also noted as potentially the fastest bird in level flight, reaching speeds of 68 miles per hour or more. Their cruising speed outperforms the famously fast Peregrine Falcon in sustained horizontal flight while hunting their preferred prey like ptarmigan and seabirds. The gyrfalcon is the world's fastest bird in level flight with an average speed of 50-68 miles per hour.

The White-throated Needletail Swift is frequently cited as the fastest bird in level (flapping) flight, with commonly reported speeds of up to 105 miles per hour. Other estimates suggest normal flying speeds of around 81 miles per hour. It is known for being a powerful flyer, distinct from the faster, diving-based records of other species. These birds are among the fastest in the world, spending most of their time in the air.

The Eurasian hobby is a small, highly agile falcon known for its incredible speed, capable of reaching speeds up to 100 miles per hour while hunting, particularly when chasing fast prey like swallows, swifts, and dragonflies. They are recognized for their remarkable mid-air acrobatics and ability to catch insects and birds on the wing. Some sources mention cruising speeds of roughly 65 miles per hour. These raptors are common in Africa, Europe, and Asia, often found in open woodlands, farmlands, and heathlands.

The Mexican free-tailed bat is one of the world's fastest mammals, capable of reaching speeds of nearly 100 miles per hour in level flight, making it faster than most birds in horizontal flight and one of the fastest mammals on Earth. They are strong flyers, often reaching altitudes over 10,000 feet while hunting insects. They achieve these speeds in horizontal, powered flight, unlike diving birds like the peregrine falcon.

Frigatebirds are incredibly fast, capable of reaching speeds up to 95 mph, making them one of the world's fastest birds. They are known for their efficient, soaring flight and ability to stay airborne for long periods of time, even sleeping while flying. They achieve this speed with powerful flight muscles and large wings relative to their body weight, using them to snatch prey from the air or water. Masters of gliding and soaring, they rarely flap their wings and can glide for long distances.

Rock Doves or Pigeons have been clocked at speeds exceeding 90 miles per hour. Their sustained flight speed averages around 40 to 60 miles per hour, but they can fly at much higher speeds if needed. Doves can maneuver and quickly change course mid-flight to escape a predator. Rock doves (pigeons) achieve high speeds due to a combination of powerful, specialized breast muscles, lightweight hollow bones, and an aerodynamic body shape with long, pointed wings.

Spur-winged geese are the fastest-flying waterfowl, capable of reaching speeds of 88 miles per hour. Native to sub-Saharan Africa, these large birds often appear on lists of top avian speed performers. They hold the record for the fastest-flying species of waterfowl. Spur-winged geese can fly at speeds up to 88 mph, achieving this remarkable pace through powerful, broad wings, heavy body weight, and efficient, long-distance muscle endurance. Their large, strong wings allow for significant lift.

The Grey-headed albatross is one of the fastest horizontal flyers, capable of reaching speeds of up to 80 miles per hour. They use a technique called dynamic soaring, allowing them to glide for long distances at high speeds without flapping their wings, often in strong wind conditions. They can maintain these high speeds for hours and have been known to travel around the globe in just over a month. They hold the Guinness Book of World Records for the fastest bird in level flight.

A hooked black marlin has been recorded stripping line off a fishing reel at 118 feet per second, that's equivalent to 80 miles per hour. Their normal swimming speeds are closer to 35 miles per hour, but they are built for explosive, short bursts of speed. Their streamlined bodies, powerful tails, and ability to slice through water make them one of the fastest fish in the world. They are large, powerful, and elusive fish, but their reputation as one of the ocean's fastest is well-earned.

Sailfish are widely considered one of the fastest fish in the ocean, with historical, often-cited estimates claiming burst speeds of up to 68 miles per hour. Their high speeds are made possible by a streamlined, torpedo-shaped body, a retractable dorsal fin ("sail") that reduces drag, and a powerful, muscular body designed for explosive, quick movements. They use their dorsal fin to corral prey, often hunting in groups to stun baitfish with their, elongated bill.

Swordfish are among the fastest fish in the ocean, capable of reaching top speeds of 60 miles per hour. Their incredible speed is due to a streamlined body, powerful tail, and a special gland at the base of their sword that secretes oil to reduce drag while they are swimming. This speed, combined with their sharp, sword-like bill, allows them to stun or injure prey, such as squid and mackerel. They are large predators, growing up to 14 feet in length and weighing over 1,000 pounds.

Yellowfin Tuna can swim at fast speeds, around 50 miles per hour. The tail of a tuna moves so fast, that it causes cavitation when it is swimming. The Tuna has bony fins without nerve endings, which prevents the fish from feeling the pain of cavitation, but does not fully protect them from the damage caused by the cavitation. A Tuna has a streamlined, torpedo-shaped body, powerful tail, and retractable fins for reduced drag when swimming. Unlike most fish, they are warm-blooded, giving them enhanced speed and endurance.

A horsefly, specifically the male, is one of the fastest insects, capable of reaching astonishing speeds up to 90 miles per hour. At 90 miles per hour, a horsefly is exceptionally fast, outperforming many other flying insects and even some land animals like cheetahs. This extreme speed is used for aerial pursuits of other insects. One study noted a male horsefly catching an air rifle pellet in midair, now that's fast.

The Southern Giant Darner or Dragonfly is regarded as one of the fastest insects, with recorded speeds often cited around 60 miles per hour. The Southern Giant Darner lives in eastern Australia and is a large, strong-flying dragonfly found along streams. They are highly agile, able to hover, fly backward, and change direction instantly. Typical, sustained flying speeds are much lower, around 15 miles per hour.

The perentie is a species of monitor lizard. It is one of the largest living lizards after the Komodo dragon. The perentie is Australia's largest monitor lizard, it can run at top speeds of 25 miles per hour. This rapid speed allows them to hunt prey and move quickly. They can run on two legs to increase speed and use their muscular tails for balance and defense. They are considered excellent endurance hunters, capable of maintaining high speeds to chase down prey such as rabbits.

Green Iguanas are large arboreal lizards capable of running at high speeds on the ground. Green iguanas can run surprisingly fast in short bursts, reaching speeds of over 22 miles per hour. This speed is used for evasion, allowing them to flee threats quickly. They utilize their long, muscular tails, which make up half their body length, for powerful thrusts and balance during these fast movements. While known for speed on land, they are also strong swimmers, able to hold their breath for extended periods of time.

Cheetahs are the fastest cats on the planet. A cheetah can run around 70 miles per hour or even faster for short bursts, making it the fastest land animal, but it can only maintain this speed for about 20-30 seconds before needing to rest due to high energy expenditure. Cheetahs are built for speed, they have a flexible spine that allows them to stretch out on each stride. Cheetahs don't roar like other big cats, they meow and purr like house cats. They also have the best eyesight of any cat.

The pronghorn (American antelope) is the fastest animal over long distances. A pronghorn can reach speeds up to 60 miles per hour, making it the fastest land animal in North America and the second-fastest globally after the cheetah, but unlike the cheetah, it can sustain these high speeds for much longer distances, relying on endurance for predator evasion. They have extra-light bones, a large heart, large lungs, and hooves designed for shock absorption, optimizing them for speed and endurance.

Springboks are highly agile antelopes capable of running at speeds of up to 56 miles per hour. Known as one of Africa's fastest land animals, they use this speed and their signature vertical, stiff-legged leaping behavior, known as pronking, to evade predators. When excited or frightened, they perform leaps up to 11.5 feet high and can cover up to 30 feet in a single bound.

The Tsessebe is recognized as one of the fastest antelope species in Africa, capable of reaching speeds up to 56 miles per hour. These animals are built for high-speed, long-distance running across open grasslands and savannas, utilizing a powerful, stretching stride to escape predators. Despite their speed, they often stop to look back at danger, which is a common, often fatal mistake.

The fastest horse speed was achieved by a Thoroughbred. On average, a horse runs at speeds between 25 and 30 miles per hour when galloping, with trained racehorses frequently hitting 40–50 miles per hour over short distances. While the fastest recorded speed is 44 miles per hour by a Thoroughbred, some Quarter Horses can reach speeds of 55 miles per hour in short sprints. Over long distances, horses maintain a much lower, averaging around 10 to 15 miles per hour.

Gazelles are exceptionally fast, with most species capable of reaching top speeds of 60 miles per hour in short bursts to evade predators. While cheetahs can out-sprint them, gazelles rely on superior endurance and agility, sustaining high speeds of 40 miles per hour over long distances and using zig-zagging, leaping techniques to escape. Gazelles are built for speed, having evolved to run on their tiptoes rather than flat feet.

Wildebeests are the largest member of the antelope family. The wildebeest exists as two species, the blue wildebeest and the black wildebeest. Both are extremely fast runners. A wildebeest can run incredibly fast, reaching top speeds of around 50 miles per hour in short bursts to escape predators, though they often maintain a slower, more sustainable pace for their long migrations. Their speed and endurance help them evade predators like lions and cheetahs, as cheetahs can only sprint for short distances.

Blackbuck antelope are small, slender, and built for speed, with males displaying long, spiraled horns. The blackbuck antelope can sustain speeds of 50 miles per hour for over 1 mile at a time. Each of its strides, the distance between its hoofprints, is 19 to 22 feet in one stride. They are also known to jump 6-7 feet in the air, a behavior known as "pronking" or "stotting," which they use to escape danger.

Hartebeest are among the fastest and most enduring African antelopes, capable of reaching speeds of up to 50 miles per hour to evade predators. They utilize a unique, zigzag running pattern when threatened, allowing them to maintain high speeds over long distances. They are known as "tough ox" due to their ability to maintain high speeds and endurance for long distances.

The impala is one of the most common and most graceful of all Africa's antelopes. An impala can reach speeds of 56 miles per hour, using its incredible agility and explosive leaps (up to three times its height) to escape predators, making them quick and elusive. The impala's key to survival relies on rapid acceleration, confusing zig-zagging motions, and massive vertical and horizontal leaps.

A female lion is called a lioness. Lionesses are smaller and more agile than males, acting as the primary hunters in the pride. Lionesses are fast and agile, reaching top speeds of 50 miles per hour in short, explosive bursts, but they lack the stamina for long distant chases, relying on stealth, teamwork, and these quick sprints to ambush prey on the African savanna. Their lighter build and lack of a heavy mane (compared to males) make them more effective hunters.

The hare or jackrabbit is bigger than a cottontail rabbit with longer ears and legs. Hares are exceptionally fast runners, typically reaching speeds of 40 miles per hour, with some species, such as the brown hare and jackrabbit, able to achieve bursts up to 50 miles per hour to escape predators. Their powerful hind legs allow for sudden, high-speed, zig-zag maneuvers, making them highly effective at evasive, fast-paced movement over open terrain. Their long, strong, and powerful hind legs enable them to jump up to 10 feet at a time.

African wild dog packs have high levels of communication with each other. The African wild dog can run up to 44mph, the same as a greyhound dog. When hunting, African wild dogs can maintain speeds of 35 miles per hour for up to 3 miles. Because of their long-distance endurance, their targeted prey rarely escapes.

Greyhounds are the fastest dogs and have primarily been bred for hunting game and racing. Greyhounds are the fastest dog breed, reaching average racing speeds over 40 miles per hour and hitting top speeds of around 45 miles per hour in short bursts, though their usual winning race pace is around 38 miles per hour. These sleek, muscular dogs accelerate incredibly fast, reaching full speed in just a few strides.

Zebras and are part of the horse family. Zebras have a home range anywhere between 11 and 232 square miles and they can travel 10 miles a day while grazing. Zebras can run at top speeds of around 40 miles per hour. They often use zigzagging, unpredictable movements to confuse attackers. Zebras have excellent stamina and can sustain fast speeds for long distances. Baby Zebras can run within hours of birth.

Eland, the largest African antelope, can run at speeds of approximately 25 to 43 miles per hour. While often cited as the slowest antelope, they can reach speeds up to 43 miles per hour. Despite their massive weight, they are highly athletic and capable of jumping from a standing start to heights of 8 to 10 feet in the air. As the largest antelope, weighing up to 2,000 pounds, their speed is considered impressive for their size.

Coyotes can adapt and live almost anywhere, even in the city. Coyotes are remarkably fast, capable of reaching top running speeds of 43 miles per hour when chasing prey or fleeing danger. They typically trot at 6 miles per hour but can sustain high-speed gallops of 30 miles per hour over long distances. They are highly agile, capable of jumping up to 14 feet in distance. They are considered the fastest member of the Canidae family in many areas, often hunting by exhausting their prey with high speeds.

Tigers are considered one of the most beautiful cats by many. The average speed of a tiger when running is between 35 to 40 miles per hour. Tigers use their speed and agility to stalk and ambush prey, often running short distances at high speeds to catch their prey. Factors that affect a tiger's running speed include its age, weight, physical condition, and the terrain it is running on.

The hyena can run up to 40 miles per hour. They use their speed to chase their prey, sometimes traveling 15 miles in a single chase. While they are often known for scavenging food, spotted hyenas are highly skilled hunters that kill 66 to 90% of their own food. Hyena's have a large heart and lungs provide them with exceptional stamina, allowing them to outlast many prey animals.

Giraffes are the tallest land animals in the world. They can run as fast as 35 miles an hour over short distances, or cruise at 10 miles per hour over longer distances. Their legs are approximately 6 feet or longer, allowing them to cover a significant amount of ground with each step. Giraffes use a specialized gait, often moving both legs on one side of the body simultaneously for stability, or galloping where they swing their hind legs outside their front legs to avoid tripping.

African buffalo are surprisingly fast, capable of reaching top speeds of 37 miles per hour, allowing them to outrun predators like lions and charge with great force despite their large size and bulk. This speed, combined with their strength and unpredictable nature, makes them one of Africa's most dangerous animals. Their aggressive defense stance contributes to their nickname, the "black death," due to the danger they pose to predators.

Rhinos are surprisingly fast, capable of running at top speeds of 30 to 40 miles per hour, with some, like the black rhino, reaching up to 40 miles per hour. Despite their immense weight, often over 2 thousand pounds, they are the fastest land mammal of that size and can accelerate quickly. They are surprisingly agile and can turn quickly despite their bulky size. Due to their poor eyesight but high speed, it is advised to climb trees to escape a charge.

The grizzly bear, often referred to as the brown bear, can reach speeds of up to 35 mph, thanks to its powerful forelegs. This puts it just ahead of the American black bear, the most widespread bear species in North America. Despite their large and muscular frames, grizzly bears are built for speed. Their distinctive shoulder humps, composed of powerful muscles, give them exceptional strength in their forelimbs, which they use for digging, climbing, and, when necessary, running.

Warthogs are surprisingly fast, capable of sprinting at speeds up to 35 miles per hour to escape predators. They often rely on this speed, along with their agility, to run for cover in burrows. They can reach these top speeds quickly over short distances. Warthogs are not just fast, they are capable of sharp, agile movements, using their tusks for defense if cornered. When fleeing, they often hold their tails straight up in the air as a warning sign to other warthogs.

Hippopotamuses can run surprisingly fast on land, reaching top speeds of approximately 20 miles per hour in short bursts or charges. Despite their massive, bulky, and short-legged frame, they can outrun most humans, often reaching these speeds over short distances. Their running gait is often described as a, sometimes becoming airborne, or as a rapid trot. Hippos love water, while they do not swim, they can move incredibly fast along the bottom of rivers and lakes, propelling themselves at high speeds.

An adult elephant can reach top running speeds of approximately 25 miles per hour. While they are capable of this high speed, it is typically used for short bursts or charging. Despite their speed, they do not jump and always keep at least one foot on the ground. Elephants move at high speeds by increasing their stride rate and length while maintaining contact with the ground. Their normal walking pace is around 4 mph.

# Author Page

Billy Grinslott – Kinsey Marie Books

Copyright, All Rights Reserved

ISBN – 9781968228552

**Thanks**

www.ingramcontent.com/pod-product-compliance
Lightning Source LLC
Chambersburg PA
CBHW060848270326
41934CB00002B/45